Amber Necklace from
GDAŃSK

poems

Linda Nemec Foster

Louisiana State University Press *Baton Rouge* 2001

10   09   08   07   06   05   04   03   02
5   4   3   2

Designer: Laura Roubique Gleason
Typeface: Minion
Typesetter: Coghill Composition Co. Inc.
Printer and binder: Thomson-Shore, Inc.

Library of Congress Cataloging-in-Publication Data

Foster, Linda Nemec.
    Amber necklace from Gdansk : poems / Linda Nemec Foster.
        p.   cm.
    ISBN 0-8071-2711-6 — ISBN 0-8071-2712-4 (pbk.)
    1. Polish Americans—Poetry.   2. Americans—Poland—Poetry.
3. Poland—Poetry.   4. Women—Poetry.   I. Title.
PS3556.O766 A82   2002
811'.54—dc21   2001002953

The author gratefully acknowledges the editors of the following publications, in which some of the poems in this book first appeared, sometimes in slightly different form: *Artful Dodge* ("Colors from the City of White," "The Rain in Bielsko"); *Atlanta Review* ("Wedding Gown Bazaar"); *The Bridge* ("Young Boy in a Tenement House, Holding the Moon"); *Calliope* ("The Silent One"); *DoubleTake* ("Gospel Eggs"); *Driftwood Review* ("The Rain Leaving Its Breath on the Grass"); *Indiana Review* ("The Awkward Young Girl Approaching You"); *International Poetry Review* ("My Mother Embracing Her Daughter in a Garden of Sunflowers"); *MacGuffin* ("For My Family," "Moje Rozwiane Włosy," "On Winning the Nobel Prize," "The Tree That Almost Died," "The Visitors from Warsaw"); *Mid-American Review* ("Mazovian Willows," "Ritual"); *Nimrod* ("Mengele's Butterflies"); *Parting Gifts* ("The Woman with the Two Rivers Growing from Her Hair"); *Passages North* ("The Therapeutist:* After Magritte"); *Pleiades* ("After the War: Purple Flowers Spilling from the Windows"); *Poet Lore* ("Amber Necklace from Gdańsk," "Our Last Day in Kraków"); *River Styx* ("Disposable Icon," "In My Grandmother's House"); *Visions International* ("Chapel with Skulls," "Fashion Statement in Front of the Palace of Culture and Science"); *Witness* ("Dancing with My Sister"); *WordWrights* ("The Two Rivers in My Story"); *Writer to Writer* ("Letter from the Last Place on Earth").

    "Amber Necklace from Gdańsk," "Dancing with My Sister," "Our Last Day in Kraków," and "Portrait of My Father, Learning to Count" were published in *New Poems from the Third Coast: Contemporary Michigan Poetry,* ed. Michael Delp, Conrad Hilberry, and Josie Kearns (Wayne State University Press, 2000). "Dancing with My Sister" was also published in *Century of Voices,* ed. Corinne Abatt et al. (Detroit Women Writers, 1999). "Sitting in America at the End of the Century" was published in *And What Rough Beast: Poems at the End of the Century,* ed. Robert McGovern and Stephen Haven (Ashland Poetry, 1999). "The Immigrant Children at Union School" was included in the essay "Creative Border Crossing in New Public Culture" by Lambert Zuidervaart, in *Literature and the Renewal of the Public Sphere,* ed. Susan VanZanten Gallagher and M. D. Walhout (Macmillan, 2000; St. Martin's, 2000).

Special acknowledgment is given to Eric Pankey for permission to quote from his poem "To Shape a Past." Also, many thanks to Ewa Lewak and Rob Burdick for assistance in manuscript preparation.
    The author wishes to thank the Arts Foundation of Michigan for a grant that was instrumental in the completion of this manuscript.

This publication is supported in part by a grant from the National Endowment for the Arts.

For My Family

For Maria with her painted toenails at the Kraków airport, exotic red
  birds ready to take flight;

For Leon in love with Polish vodka, Italian cars, his own moustache, rac-
  ing the wind through the hills of yellow light south of any town blur-
  ring past;

For Agnieszka with her necklace of worn pencils, written words nubbed
  to the bone in a halting foreign language;

For Monika in love with a boy in California whose ex-girlfriend stops
  her on a Bielsko street to complain about rain, the advantage of being
  the sky;

For Paweł with his red hair, loud rock music in a small car, pissing on
  the side of the road and proclaiming it a new venture in capitalism;

For Michał's long, silent hair and slow wave of good-bye, a soldier's
  white flag of surrender;

For Father Antoni's dark church, large oak carved into a Madonna, who
  forgets to pray unless prompted by the fog;

For Father Józef who went to Rome to visit Keats' grave and not the
  Pope, who recites Shakespeare as if it were a cascading stream falling
  from his mouth;

For Anna who touches my American face like it's Braille and she could
  read with her hands my mother's lavender room, my father's small
  garden;

For Stanisław with his one arm and brown suit, new house with four
  chairs in the living room, no wife in sight;

For Krystyna who kisses icons of the Black Madonna as if they were inti-
  mate friends, whose husband is busy in Germany making money,
  who peels diamonds for dessert;

For Elżbieta whose husband is a ghost that sits at the table and demands
  strong tea, only the good china, bleached lace tablecloth;

For Michael, my secret lover, offering soft rain instead of flowers, the
  beautiful gray of Nowy Sącz, his hand, his voice lost in my hair;

For Hanka and her tentative smile wanting the sparrows to stay quiet, all
  her words swallowed like plum wine;

For Łukasz who can see breasts with closed eyes, the constellations of
  form that spiral the galaxy, the economy, the neighbor's backyard;

For Jakub, his brother and comrade in closed eyes, astrophysics, free-
  market initiatives that grow like grass knocking at the front door;

For Marta, cat-girl, taking "MEOW" to new heights of European simplic-
  ity: *tak* or *nie*, yes or no;

For Father Bronisław with his white surplice recently washed by the rain,
who knows all the names of my Cleveland relatives by heart—the
dead and the living—spinster cousins who say novenas to greenhouse
orchids;

For the anonymous cousin in Niskowa who lives in a white room, ceiling
and walls covered in ivy, the air thick with green, her granddaughter's
face filled with nothing but thin tendrils of the family tree.

Contents

IV. To Smile at the Closed Mouth of Loss

Somewhere between description of a landscape
And the landscape described, we fell asleep.

Begin *I remember* and the faded world,
The relinquished world, returns only as dream.

—Eric Pankey, "To Shape a Past"

I   Conjuring Up the Landscape

The Awkward Young Girl Approaching You

for Gary Gildner

Who will speak for the dispossessed,
those who come from nowhere,
whose birthplace cannot be found
on any map, whose muted eyes
greet us like yesterday's unread newspaper?

The man with the raw hand
in his crotch, making eye contact.
The woman with her nervous walk
piercing through traffic with her dismantled
face: blue left cheek, right eye gone
but not closed. Empty red socket
fixed at the back of your neck.

And though you remind yourself
they are not you, they are
with you everywhere. On the street,
on a bus, in the darkest corner
of last night's dream. Even traveling
to the country of your grandfather,
the country he left before being displaced,
cannot protect you from their stares.

In Katowice, the grayest city
in the grayest part of the world,
you are not prepared for the awkward
young girl approaching you. She
is not pretty and her hair is not clean
like America but she shimmers in her
pale yellow dress and dyed-to-match
satin pumps. She is trying to be beautiful
and you are not ready for her smile that
reminds you of every single thing you've ever lost.

And the way her golden feet attempt
to walk on Katowice's gray and broken

cobblestones stirs a memory that only
your dead grandfather could understand:
wildflowers overrunning the garden, cicadas
drowning out the factory's nightly lament.
So much grace in her graceless yellow feet.
So much of the miraculous in her thin silhouette.

As if the Black Madonna had unlocked herself
from her demanding son, left the gilded frame
of Częstochowa, and appeared before you:
asking to see your passport, evidence
that you came from somewhere, that you exist.
Dumbfounded, could you prove yourself?
Or would you become another outline,
another vague face the landscape conjured up?

Doppelgänger

Somewhere she must exist. My other self,
lost twin I've never met, only imagined:
the mirrored image of a familiar stranger.

Smoking a cigarette in a Kraków bar,
walking along a gray dock in Gdańsk,
hanging laundry in a cramped yard—anywhere

between the Tatra Mountains and Baltic Sea.
A mere roll of the dice that I'm here
and she's somewhere else, someone else

with my face, pale skin, hair streaked
blonde on brown. So many of my family
decided to stay in the Old World

it's amazing I cropped up in the New.
Surrounded by microwaves, CD-ROMs,
enough guilt to fill a baseball field

because of a simple act of birth that placed me
in the suburbs south of Cleveland and
not in a town across the river from Oświęcim.

A toast to my other half: may we each have
a long life on opposite sides of the world;
may we never recognize each other on the street.

The Therapeutist: After Magritte

The blank man offers
no answers, only memory:
the evolution of our torsos
from bird cages; how the bright
idea of heaven grew out
of the cavity of our mouths;
how gossip had its humble
origin in the pitch
of our stomach's growl.

After every theory, he offers
props so recognizable we
don't even bother to look.
The sky continues to be blue,
the ocean settles into its
grayness, the brown earth
reconciles its sullen face.

Still he's part of the landscape,
half there and half not.
Like a double exposure torn
between the mirror and chair,
the white arc of thigh
and empty sleeve. His face
resembling the cloud
that permeates the heart
when an intruder stalks it.

The Immigrant's Dream

It's a recurrent dream and in it I am lost.
I try to speak, but no words leave my lips.
I know I should be somewhere but don't know
where that is. My ears hear a woman's
voice which is at once comforting
and menacing. She speaks in whispers,
in slow, deliberate words. I cannot see her.
I learn to take nothing for granted.

It's a recurrent dream and in it I have no family.
I watch mothers, fathers, sons, and daughters
all walk by without giving me a single glance,
a single word. I forgive each of them
their abandonment. I have no hatred, no malice.
Everyone else in the dream says I should.

It's a recurrent dream and in it I fear
that it won't end, not even when I wake.
I move carefully around the dream's edge
as if it were a tiger's eye dilated
to nothing but black. I feel
a gentle but cold wind on my face.
The woman's voice whispers: You're home.

My Name

Little-known facts about my life live
inside my name, that
name I was given and the one I
decided to give myself. Against
all odds, the three words that define my
name come from languages as diverse as
English, Spanish, a blur of Slavic
meaning that no one seems to remember.
Even in dreams, my name
can assume various disguises:
flamenco dancer in tight red, satin black
or a soft breeze that defies the invading army.
See how its borders shift as easily as its vowels.
The name transplanted in the waking world
echoes the sound of a child's footsteps at dusk
retracing, with care and doubt, the long way home.

Young Boy in a Tenement House, Holding the Moon

He is as anonymous as a fairy tale.
His bare feet could be my father's
or perhaps my son's: narrow and
delicate, their stance casual
like the worn floorboards underneath.
His thin arms hold a chipped basin
under a cracked spigot—no sink,
no drain, no luxury of hot and cold—
just an exposed faucet growing
out of the wall. How patient
he is, waiting for the spigot
to speak "water" no matter how
turbid or unclear the response.
His shorn hair, free of lice;
his too loose clothing that will
never quite fit. Try to ignore
what you can't see anyway:
his mother five flights up
keeping six kids at bay, waiting
for that basin of water as if
it could wash everything away.
The boy's hands cup the white rim
like a halo, a pale nimbus. He smiles
not for the camera, but to himself,
as if he's holding a captured moon
and whispering to it, his breath
lost in its silver and dust:
księżyc, księżyc, latać, latać, daleko.
Moon, moon, fly away, fly away,
and please, take me with you.

Portrait of My Father, Learning to Count

He is barely two, pale and shy, this boy
who sits at the kitchen table in a house
filled with oak and mahogany, foreign words,
the smell of black bread. He is waiting
for his mother as casually as he waits for the sun
every morning to steal quietly into his room.

She is late, but he sits patiently in this room,
his small fingers play games like those of any boy.
Here's the church, here's the steeple, as the day's sun
falls behind the lace curtain. The house
sinks into the sounds of evening: hushed breeze waiting,
holding its breath. Until finally she enters with words

of apology, hushed accents of Silesia. *Janek.* The word
that speaks his name and fills the entire room
like a boundless echo. Her voice repeating it and waiting
for his hesitant reply. And, again, saying the boy's
name as if to convince herself he is here, alive, in a house
in America that not even the wind or rain or sun

in Poland could imagine. How to tell the American sun,
"thank you, thank you," when most of the words
she knows are so weighted with syllables the house
starts to forget them. But not the boy in this room.
He will remember because he is the first son, a quiet boy
whose father sweats in a factory, whose mother waits

at the woolen mill for piecework. Their lives waiting
for their son to be something better and not working in sun-
baked fields outside Zielona Góra, a green place the boy
will never see. *Nic starego, jedynie nowe.* Quietly the words
leave her lips: nothing old, only new. As if the room
could eavesdrop and for a long moment everything does: the house,

damask tablecloth, even the bare trees touching the dark house's
outline. On the table, she places her day's wages and waits
for him to begin. *Jeden, dwa, trzy.* A chant that lifts the room

to heaven. But she doesn't want heaven, only America: its sun-
light, shadow, brick streets, thin dirt. He says the wrong words
again and again until finally he pleases her. The small boy

with his *one, two, three* filling the room. And even the sun
lingers a bit to hear. The house changes with the sound, waits.
One, two, three. Words falling like dusk around her American boy.

Immigrant Children at Union School

We come from Bratislava and Wrocław,
Budapest and Prague, Minsk and Tulcea:
a veritable United Nations in my kinder-
garten class. Our halting English
frustrates the teacher but never our-
selves—we know what we're trying to say.
We color and paint and draw and listen
to a story read aloud about a missing
princess and the poor peasant boy
who must find her. All the girls
want to be the princess, all the boys
want to be the peasant. I just want
to be here in America, in Ohio,
in Cleveland, living on Salem Avenue
four houses from my grandparents,
and walking to Union School every
morning holding my grandfather's
right hand. In other words, I hardly want
anything else. But maybe three things:
to be smart enough to read English
and brave enough to scold that princess
for getting lost and kind enough not
to make fun of the girl from Hungary
with the bright red ribbon in her hair
who always draws her cats with eight legs.

The Old Neighborhood

In the mid-sixties, when the Cuyahoga River
periodically caught on fire, my hometown
of Cleveland became the butt of national jokes.
"Ha, ha," laughed Johnny Carson and everyone
laughed right along. Everyone, that is,
except the people who lived in Cleveland.

"They're calling us The Mistake on the Lake,"
Annie Slodowski said as we walked to school
one morning. "Who's 'they'?" I asked.
"You know. Johnny Carson. The people on TV.
The rest of the country. Living in Cleveland
is a real drag. I think I'll move."

I knew this was an empty threat, since Annie
and her family would never move; not only
was she stuck in Cleveland, but stuck
in that particular neighborhood off Broadway
and East 69th. Her father was the only butcher
for blocks; business was too good to move anywhere else.

Slodowski's Butcher Shoppe on Broadway
was a real feast for the senses.
The creaking wooden floors were covered with sawdust,
the cooler was stuffed with fresh meat,
her father's white apron splattered with the day's work.
"The dirtier, the better," he'd tell Annie.
I loved to visit and smell the fresh kielbasa
and czarnina, the cow's tongue and blood sausage.
Besides, Annie and her family lived
in an apartment above the store. What a paradise,
I thought. Why move because some pencil-thin
comedian in New York gives your town a bum rap?

Actually—and I couldn't admit this to Annie—
I loved Cleveland and the old neighborhood
and I didn't even live in an exotic place like she did.
Our house—or more correctly, the upper flat
we lived in—was on Salem Avenue, right before
it dead-ended into East 69th. We lived four houses

from my grandparents', which was the closest thing
to heaven, as far as I was concerned, and right above
Pat the Mechanic (Pat as in Patrick), who fixed cars.

The narrow street was paved with red bricks,
filled with kids playing kickball and freeze tag.
Their mothers and fathers were first- or second-
generation immigrants from Poland, Bohemia,
Hungary, Slovakia, and Lithuania. Their names
reflected the geography of their history:
Blaszak, Zayti, Solinski, Majkrzak, Stefaniuk.
All Slavic, with pale, broad faces attached to each name.
And everyone knew everybody else. A blessing
and a curse, my mother would sigh under her breath,
when our neighbor Mrs. Krenek asked her when
she was going to have another baby.

As I drifted off to sleep at night, I often heard
my parents talk about the neighbors in hushed whispers.
Kosmarek the Drunk,
Polumski the Wise Guy with the Barking Dog,
Horvath the Creep.
This litany in English would ultimately drift
into one in Polish: *dzika świnia, brudna świnia,
dziki Amerykanin.* Wild pig, dirty pig, wild American.

These litanies were as essential to the landscape
of my childhood as the names of streets—
Grand Division, Kinsman, Daveney—or the names
of neighborhoods—Ducktown, Slavic Village, the Flats.
No other city in the world had these names.
They might have their own, but none that sounded
like a hundred pennies in my pocket or that fell
from my lips like sweet, dark plum juice.
And though I never told anyone—especially not
Annie Slodowski—I was secretly excited
to be living in the City of the Flaming River.

The Silent One

My mother never told me fairy tales.
They frightened her and she was certain
they were true: fabulous beasts that talked
and, by a word, changed themselves into men;
magnificent castles that became thin clouds;
evil sorcerers that turned straw into gold
and dried dandelions into dead children.

She remembered the stories her grandmother told
but tried to forget them, always wondering
if she wasn't someone else—an untamed
firebird covered in jewels, a princess
bewitched into marrying the wrong man.

My mother was afraid. Afraid that once she
spoke the tales to the air, the air
would listen and bind them to her.
All the foul-smelling monsters, gnarled
witches. But also those handsome princes,
magic gowns, fiery necklaces encased in ice.
For her, these tales of beauty were the most
dangerous: soft words that enticed,
that seduced, but kept her at a distance.

My mother refused to speak the words
of myth, of the small hidden heart
waiting to be discovered. I tried
to discover it myself—in the wind
moaning at my window, in the tired
branches trying to reinvent the sky,
in the singing moon that found my eyes
wide with brown, blue, green. Colors
of earth, heaven, ocean. My eyes
the same colors as hers, the silent one.

Ritual

Every year the ritual was hauled out
with the faded dungarees and red
flannel shirts, the hiking boots
and old caps. The men in my family
called it the ritual of mushroom-
picking or luck in northern Ohio.

These men—my grandfather, father,
and three uncles—allowed only
one female on their daylong journey
into the woods. Me. The good luck
charm. And at five, entering the woods
at Tinkers Creek with them for the first
time, what did I know of luck? How
it could elude you forever or come
crashing down just inches from
your startled face like a jagged
question mark, a broken tree limb?

What I did know was the damp
scent of crushed pine needles
under my father's boot, quiet fragrance
of green leaves turning from themselves
into the season: veins of red,
canopy of yellow, floor of brown.

What I did know was the coarse feel
of the burlap sack in my hand,
how it became heavy with mushrooms.
Plucking the stalk delicately so it
wouldn't crumble in my hand. Telling
the difference between destroying
angel and scarlet head, white morel
and shaggymane. Fingering the soft
pleated gills underneath the cap, wanting
to kiss that softness, the deep velvet.

Toward the end of the day, when I
became tired, the men left me
next to a huge oak while they went

deeper into the woods. I was alone
with only the brown leaves at my feet
ready to rise up and devour me;
familiar calls of sparrow, jay, crow
becoming screams. Thin and strange.

And the luck, the real luck of that day
was not that I never moved an inch
from where they left me. Or that I never
cried out. My luck was they came back
for me, those large looming men
with their Slavic faces, thick hands.
Their one act of deliverance bringing
them luck, bringing me back to my bed.
And the smell of cooked morels, melted
butter, strong onions. Common voices
of men as they reinvented the day.

The Tree That Almost Died

When I was a young girl growing up in Cleveland,
there was an old tree in my grandparents' backyard
that almost died. My grandfather couldn't let it go—
this oak that had become diseased and blighted.
It had a huge gap on its side where parasites,
a slow litany of insects and their larvae,
had eaten away the bark through the pulp
to the very core of the tree.

"*Oucu, oucu, rana,*" he said when I asked what it was.
His Polish words for "hurt," "sore," or "oweee"
as my three-year-old mind would translate.
He was determined to bring the tree back:
to have it alive and flourishing in the summer,
silent and sleeping in the winter. From his American
garden and his Polish memory, he made a poultice,
a healing salve. A Secret, he said whenever
I asked him what the mixture was made of.

One afternoon he and I smoothed the salve
over the tree's wound touching the inside pulp.
"Look, Leenda, *ładna dziewczyno*, pretty girl,
the silent heart of the tree." Although impossible,
I wanted to be able to count the rings to see how old
it was; I imagined it to be as old as my father.

All the time we worked on the tree, caressing
it with our salve-covered fingers, my grandfather
spoke softly in Polish. Not to me, but to the tree:
śpij, śpij, nie troskaj się—sleep, sleep, don't worry.
Little words that sounded like the village
in southern Silesia he left and never saw again.

After we finished with the salve, we put a huge
dressing on the gap. Clean, white strips of cloth
that we wound around the trunk like a big bandage.
"Now what?" I asked my *dziadek*. "We wait."

It took two years, a lifetime for me, but the tree
healed completely. All the neighbors marveled;

even my grandmother was impressed. Still, Grandpa
refused to tell anyone The Secret, what he mixed
together in the back shed to make the salve.
For me, the real healing power came from his words,
his thick foreign words that wafted like incense
in and around the tree and straight up to heaven.

Twelve years after the tree came back to life,
my *dziadek* died. Then his wife, my *babcia,* five years
later. Their house—the only house they lived in
here in America—eventually became run-down and decrepit
like the dying inner-city neighborhood surrounding it.

But the oak tree is still standing: baptized with green
leaves every spring, frozen in bareness every winter.
You can hardly see where the *oucu* was. All smooth
except for a tiny scar that looks like the crescent
moon. White, luminescent. *Dobry, dobry.*
Good, good, *dziadek* would say. A little of ourselves
left behind so the tree won't forget us.

The Countries That Claim Me

I am from America and Poland.
I wonder how I came to have hazel eyes:
flecks of earth, sky, and sea in my gaze.
I hear the low pitch of the moon
as it swings above the roof.
I see crows, their blue-black emblem of regret.
I want to touch that regret, to kiss it.

I pretend to be a cloud, a shadow,
a figment of some distant past.
I feel lucky and American, Polish and cursed.
I touch the old and the new—mother, daughter.
I worry about not really knowing either.
I cry because my son will never dance
the mazurka, polonaise, *oberek.*
I am from America and Poland.

I understand English—nothing more.
I say it is not enough, not enough.
I dream in a foreign language thick
with the sound of dark trees.
I try to translate the words of each leaf.
I hope the wind will carry my response.
I am from America and Poland.

Sitting in America at the End of the Century

I am stuck in a typical five o'clock traffic jam
in a nondescript city in the nation's great
midsection near the end of the hyperbolic,
twentieth century. The car's cassette player
holds a tape from Berlitz—the fast-action
language people—and from the speakers,
wafting through the air like invisible incense,
comes a thick, guttural commotion of sounds
that first rose from that flat plain
on the other side of the world called Poland.

It's a language my grandparents never forgot,
a language my parents refused to remember
on their way to becoming total Americans.
I am stunned by the foreignness of it and
I don't mean just foreign—but alien—not
an immigration agency term—but alien—
as in Venus, Mars, something otherworldly,
exotic, not of this planet.
At least, my side of it.

This language astonishes and frightens me
like the automated laughing lady
distorted by mirrors in the fun house.
The blurred image of a face I know,
but can't quite recognize—vertigo
of awkward beauty and boundary and color.

I try to repeat the innocuous phrasing . . .

What is that?   *Co to jest?*

Can I get some milk?   *Czy mozna tu dostać mleko?*

I am lost.   *Zabładziłem.*

Thank you, Mrs. Falska.   *Dziekuję, Pani Falska.*

All the while remembering my grandparents,
Maria and Tomasz, Zofia and Franciszek,

at the other end of the century—the wild,
promising beginning of it. They all left Poland
at the same time, mere strangers in a sea
of strangers. No English dictionary, no easy-
to-play cassette tape. Just one suitcase
and eighteen dollars in their collective pockets.
Moving headlong into another century,
another country, and not once looking back.

How could they know that nine decades later
the century would come to its finale like this?
A distant granddaughter surrounded by cars,
longing for a language that's more akin to damp
earth than linguistics, stuttering in a tongue
so natural to them they know what she's trying
to say, even before the halting words
leave her lips. *Bardzo mi przykro,
nie wiem.* I am sorry, I know nothing.

The Two Rivers in My Story

CUYAHOGA

The river's name sounds like a chant
and it probably is. An ancient Indian
chant born in northern Ohio when it
wasn't called Ohio but Place of Green
Water, Place of Tiny Gorges Where Trees
Come to Be Born. The chant floats
along the river's steady current
as the waters twist through gray rocks,
yellow earth, and leaning trees
like a snake wrapping around itself
until it slithers into Lake Erie
and becomes uncoiled and silent.

VISTULA

Who could not fall in love
with the name of a river that sounds
like water? Caressing the air
that leaves your mouth with such moist
nonchalance it takes your breath away.
River that is half woman, half fish:
mermaid that seduces all or nothing,
her song the last fragment you hear
before the current sweeps you away.
Imagine her as a young child, the object
of desire as virgin, as the unexplored
heart. Nothing in her veins but melted snow.

The Woman with the Two Rivers Growing from Her Hair

Here is a true story stranger than any fiction. I know it's true because my mother told me that her mother saw it with her own two eyes. The "it" was a woman—young, beautiful—who had two rivers growing from her hair. She was from Kraków and as a girl would weave her long, yellow hair into two heavy braids. They looked like twin strands of gold. *"Praw-dziwe złoto."* Real gold, my grandmother would say. But that was long ago in the old country when the woman's hair was still only hair. Although she was very beautiful—with her hair as rich as a sunset, skin as pale as sweet milk, and eyes as green as deep emeralds—she was very sad because no man seemed to be able to fall in love with a girl whose hair looked like gold. As a matter of fact, all the men and boys who ever met her felt uncomfortable in her presence. They were so awestruck by her hair that they never noticed anything else—including *her!* So she longed for a better, happier life. One day she decided to leave her mother, her father, all her sisters and brothers, aunts, uncles, cousins, and friends and come to the New World and live in America. It was difficult to say good-bye to the only life she had ever known, but she knew it would be even more difficult to stay in a place that would constantly remind her of lost love. The journey by steamship across the vast blue expanse of the Atlantic was long, hard, and lonely. But finally, she arrived in New York and made her way across that state and Pennsylvania to northern Ohio. She settled in Cleveland because she liked the way the foreign sound of the word left her Slavic lips. She especially loved the sound of the city's river, Cuyahoga, even though it took her many weeks before she could even begin to pronounce it. "Cuyahoga," she said, "Cuyahoga." As if trying to will the river into her tiny bedroom on the third floor of Mrs. Okasin-ski's boarding house. One night there was a terrible storm. Thunder rolled, lightning flashed, rain fell from the sky in endless torrents. That night the woman tossed and turned in her bed—she dreamt a strange dream. She was a mermaid swimming in the deep, clear waters of her homeland, the Vistula River. Her legs had turned into one huge fin, her beautiful hair had become filmy seaweed. Even her green eyes had turned into the blue-white of mother-of-pearl. The Vistula flowed around her like scattered diamonds. For the first time since leaving Po-land, she felt homesick. In the morning when she awoke, the rain was still falling, like drops of a river from the sky. Her pillow was damp —not from the dream, not from the tears of homesickness she cried in her sleep—but from her hair. Her long, golden hair had inexplicably transformed into the two rivers she loved so much: blue Vistula of the fish-maid; green Cuyahoga of the exotic song. They flowed from her head like twin cascades of the past and present, the old and the new. Where could she go, with her hair like rivers, what could she do? It was impossible to go home to Poland, it was impossible to stay in Cleveland, it was impossible to be a woman from both sides of this earth, trying to hold it down. Some say the woman disappeared into the rivers that claimed her. Some say she walked into the rain and became the rain. And some refuse to believe that a woman's hair can change into the waters of two rivers by a mere act of a strange dream. But then, they don't know the woman. And they don't know the woman who first told the story: Maria, my mother's mother with the green eyes who died long ago, whom I never knew, but could only imagine.

Mengele's Butterflies

On the red-eye overnight Lufthansa flight nonstop from Chicago to
Frankfurt, I am surrounded by the clipped staccato of German. And I
am reminded of my name—my real maiden name—Niemiec, which is
Polish for German. Linda Niemiec, Linda Deutsch, Linda German. A guy
from Albany, New York, once told me the mythical origins of my name.
When the mainly Slavic tribes were confronted for the first time by Ger-
manic tribes, they, of course, couldn't understand what was being said.
The Germans tried speaking louder and wildly gesticulating; they
thought that this would get their ideas across. The Slavs just thought the
Germans were mad or maybe deaf and couldn't hear a thing without
shouting. So *niemiec* has its roots in the word *mute* for the Slavic lan-
guages—at least that's what the guy in Albany told me. And maybe that's
why Hitler and Stalin ultimately never hit it off, despite that bankrupt
nonaggression pact they signed in 1939. The pact that signaled the begin-
ning of the end for Poland and, in a larger sense, for Germany and Rus-
sia, too. I think Hitler always suspected Stalin of being a Jew. As a matter
of fact, he even had his official state photographer go to Moscow (before
Hitler ever met Stalin) and take closeup photos of Stalin's earlobes to see
if they were connected (*i.e.* Aryan) or disconnected and separate (*i.e.*
Jewish), according to the current racial theories espoused by the Nazis.
The photographer did his job—with complete discretion, of course—
and Hitler pronounced Stalin's earlobes connected and Aryan. So Slavic
ears were spared, but not Slavic eyes. The notorious Angel of Death at
Auschwitz, Dr. Josef Mengele, had a fascination for Jewish and Slavic
eyes (along with his obsession for twins). Blue and brown were beautiful
but too commonplace. What really excited him was the rare hazel and
even rarer green. On the wall of his office at Auschwitz were meticulous
rows of colors that rivaled gorgeous butterflies. Their colors an array of
variations of blue, brown, green, violet, black. Their colors created from
the preserved irises of his victims. Eyes of the Jew from Warsaw, the Pole
from Tarnów, the Gypsy from Budapest, the homosexual from Prague.
And I think of my mother's mother with her jet black hair and olive skin:
looking not Slavic or Germanic but different. As if Hitler with his pen-
chant for earlobes could uncover the secret of what it is that sets us apart
from one another. My mother's mother who looked different enough to
be noticed, leaving for America before the Holocaust began—her skin
on her back, her green eyes alive and intact.

Layover in Frankfurt

Devoid of joy. That's how I would describe the Frankfurt airport. It's an odd mix of Orwellian gray and barren glass, steel, and chrome. All very efficient-*looking* but intimidating. And, in the final analysis, NOT user-friendly. We arrive at an older terminal —it's crazy and hectic. Hordes of people walking around dazed and confused, trying to find out where they're supposed to go next. The French woman with her blond hair in a tight bun who can't find the baggage claim; a tall young man in a rumpled raincoat holding a putting iron for a cane and doing it so casually he looks as if he's ready to golf. All the people huddled around the big schedule board that flips around continuously changing Paris into Berlin into Amsterdam, numbers into letters, time present to time future. All in a flash of an eye. We discover that we're in the wrong terminal and have to find our way to Terminal 2 using the Skyline—a slow monorail with a disembodied female voice directing you on and off in German, French, English, Spanish, and Japanese. To get to the monorail platform, we have to go through this eerie, stark, long hallway that seems to be bereft of any sound: even our voices are absorbed, snatched up by the endless black floor, the long corridor that doesn't seem to go anywhere. At least the first terminal was alive—people looked jet-lagged and glazed, but there were people. The new terminal is quite spacious and attractive but it's empty and strange. All I can think of is *1984* or, better yet, Terry Gilliam's *Brazil,* with all those mazes of tubes leading . . . leading to more tubes. We have a long layover, so for six hours we're surrounded by huge, empty space; a loud and incessant overhead voice that announces every arrival, every departure in the same dull monotone; and we have jet lag. My body is so drained of any segment of a cogent thought that I might as well be on Mars. I feel disconnected and weightless. On top of all this, we have an awful lunch at an airport restaurant ominously called "The American Bar." It's filled with quirky representations of things American: Pabst Blue Ribbon signs in neon blue; the Marlboro Man looking tough and bored; and, in front of the restaurant, teasing patrons with a pleated, white dress (à la her costume in the famous air vent scene in *The Seven-Year Itch*), is a tired, blond mannequin impersonating Marilyn Monroe. The place's accouterments are better than the food. Thin lentil soup, salty meatloaf, and (what else?) sauerkraut and sad frankfurters which look like someone's skinny intestines. Not that I had a *totally* bad experience at the Frankfurt airport, just an out-of-body one. Note the aforementioned reference to Mars. Plus my deep excitement/anxiety/fear/elation/trepidation about going to Poland. You get the scrambled picture. But now we're on the LOT Airlines flight to Kraków—the last leg of our long, long journey. The houses and farmlands, plains and hills are rushing up to meet us. Soon I'll be on Polish soil for the first time; almost one hundred years after my four grandparents left this Old World to come to the New. I'm the stranger surrounded by the foreign language of her ancestors, the voluntary exile going home.

Homecoming

Not the Polish neighborhood in Cleveland, not my grandparents with their broken English, or their children displaced in their immigrant dreams. Not the weddings at the Polish Falcon Hall on Broadway or the funerals at St. Stanislaus' cavernous church. Nothing in my diluted American past can compare with the Poland that is now below my feet, the Poland that I could never envision even in dreams. We land on the outskirts of the airport at Kraków —actually, near a military base. We all climb aboard an old pre-glasnost bus and as we pass the guards in khaki and camouflage, I feel like I've landed right in the middle of the cold war. The buildings are run-down, dilapidated, but such character. We pass a multitiered wall that sports an orange tile Spanish roof. A wall with a roof, nothing else. We pass groups of young men in uniform all peering intently into the moving bus. Probably more on the lookout for good-looking foreign women than foreign agents. We pass weeds and Queen Anne's lace choking a yard—and one solitary pine tree standing (almost) in defiance. We see a wooden well that a young boy with a red hat drinks from, cupping the water from the brown pail. We pass rows and rows of poplars that hold their stance as seriously as the cypresses near the Roman catacombs. The landscape of this military base looks almost otherworldly. Broken and old with its faded equipment in garages, its soldiers with their cocked hats and straining necks. After whipping through several checkpoints, the bus finally gets to the airport's main (and only) terminal. It's only now that we realize why we landed so far from the main gate: there's a massive construction project going on that is totally revamping the entire runway system. So that's why the crazy bus ride through the Warsaw Pact. We wait for our luggage and, lo and behold, it arrives from the depths of the baggage area in the basement. All three bags make their way up the conveyer ramp to our sweaty hands—all the way from Grand Rapids to Kraków. A miracle. But the biggest miracle awaits us on the other side of the door from customs. My cousin Maria, her daughter Agnieszka, and Agnieszka's boyfriend, Martin, are waiting for us with smiles, hugs, and flowers. Agnieszka looks absolutely beautiful—dyed red hair, a small silver stud in her nostril, a necklace made from the used stubs of pencils her brother wrote with in school. And Maria, her chestnut hair, broad face, full lips, painted toenails. The whole scene is exhilarating and overwhelming. We hug, kiss, laugh, try to communicate in our broken languages. A family separated by an ocean and ninety years sees its mirrored image for the first time. They load us (and all our baggage) into a friend's (Marek's) car, which will take us to the hotel. Marek drives like a bat out of hell: Mario Andretti transplanted onto winding Polish roads. The buildings on Kraków's outskirts may look tired, but not the people. Young boys on their bikes, lovers kissing at intersections and fountains. Marek speaks no English but knows his prayers—there's a rosary (not fuzzy dice) hanging from his rearview mirror. His prayers work because we arrive at our hotel, The Forum, in one piece. The city is alive and peaceful, active yet sedate. Our view from the room's balcony is quite spectacular—the *best* room with a view we've ever had. We can see Wawel Castle, church spires from the Old Town square, and connecting it all—the lovely Vistula. Winding past our hotel window, looking like pure glass (even with its pollution)—a perfect mirror reflecting the darkening air that colors the sky just after dusk. The moon is full and finds a home on the Vistula's waters. Bicyclists with their bike lights on look as if they're actually floating on the water, instead of riding beside it. The curving Vistula that flows through the heart of this city, this country, lifeline of my grandmother's upturned palm.

III DARK AMBER OF REGRET

Mazovian Willows
Chopin's Nocturne, Opus 9

> What has happened to my heart? I can
> hardly remember how they sing at home.
> —CHOPIN

Did the strain of a mazurka
split you in two? Don't
tell me lightning, wind,
harsh betrayal of nature—
anything that has logic.
As much logic as a Polish
composer with a French name
who wrote scores of music
for a single instrument;
who was in love with a strong
woman that adopted a man's
name because she liked
simplicity. No logic there,
old tree, stark willow.
You probably gave Frédéric
his inspiration: one
note at a time drowning out
the sky, changing your life
from a single vision
to a double one. A split
trunk resembling a pair
of hands in prayer, bruised
fingers of the émigré. Your
country not even listed
on the map. Perhaps it wasn't
a mazurka that cut your
heart in two: one side
listing to the West, the other
firmly planted in Mazovia,
despite itself.

Perhaps it was a simple
nocturne, the last fading
light before night comes
and eyes close. Music
of good-bye, farewell;
the knowledge of never
going home again. Music
of exile that almost forgets
the language of the earth.

In My Grandmother's House

Too much magenta in my grandmother's house,
magenta on my lips, cheeks, and dress:
a foreign color that doesn't belong
in this small, whitewashed hut surrounded
by earth, rain, and the green hills
of Poland. When she was born here
over a hundred years ago, this color
probably wasn't invented yet
by the dye merchant who dreamed
a battlefield of purplish red fabric and
came up with a new fashion craze. No fashion
here. Only the color of the hard dirt floor
as it breathes the air of the icon
on the wall: doleful Madonna, her blue
heart pierced with seven daggers. All gray
and breathless like eyes watching my every
American move. Too much magenta for this
place where cows and chickens live
in the next room; where my great-grandmother
froze to death in January of '29
just yards from the front door, falling
near the woodpile, falling with no one
home to help her back inside. Too much
magenta on my lips as they form
the obligatory "O" in sadness, in grief
for the woman whose name I didn't
even know until that moment. Too much
magenta on my cheeks as they are brushed
with kisses not once, or twice, but three
times by my great-aunt Anna and her one-
armed son who still live there. Afraid
to move into a modern house for fear
they'll die with indoor plumbing and no
animals. Too much magenta in my dress
that is touched by the rain in spite of
my cousin Michael's umbrella. Jagged
black ripped from a broken spoke. Too much
magenta reflecting off the glass frame
holding the sepia wedding picture of my

grandmother and grandfather, newly Americanized
in Cleveland, no going back to southern
Poland, to the hills of Doły. Until
their granddaughter returns to this house
as if she were a sleepwalker who dreams
of a world in black and white where
everything is sharp and in focus and
the clear rain fits quietly in her hand.

The Rain Leaving Its Breath on the Grass
Białowieża National Park

There is such a tentative
heart the rain reveals
every time it reaches the earth
and stays for a while.

In the early hours of a gray
afternoon, it leaves its breath
on every single thing it touches:
azaleas, violets, ivy bleeding
into the nesting maple. Rain,
falling into the long grasses
of summer, abandons the imprint
of its tenuous shadow, the quiet
breath that requires each blade
to bend down and listen
to its own true heart.

Where else on earth
would you need such total
obedience, such honesty
than in the rain?

Even the blind, gray clouds
know this and never refuse
the rain anything. Their formless
shapes—a perfect home
for the stranger that keeps leaving.

Mother Embracing Her Daughter
in a Garden of Sunflowers
Tarnów, Poland

We can't see their faces
as our rented Fiat rushes
out of their frame of reference:
an ironic day in August
filled with cold damp, the fog
cocooning every tree and streetlight.
This must be how Lenin saw art
in this part of the world—separate
and muffled. Even the dark, wooden
church is fair game, and the huge radio
antenna next to it. A socialist
joke pretending to be a long finger
questioning the heavens. But why
are they standing so close together
as if abandoned by the fog and holding
on to each other for dear life?
The mother, middle-aged and beyond
bearing children; the daughter, quietly
hiding her new breasts; and the sunflowers
with their long green necks, drooping
round faces, ready to witness
just about anything. Birth, death,
the false pretense of social realism.

The Rain in Bielsko
Bielsko-Biała, Poland

Men working
waist-deep in the ground
tunneling for
not gold or silver,
only brown water.

Three times
we pass
her statue. Mermaid
abandoned in bronze,
no sea to embrace.

City square
designed by a short man
from Vienna.
As if foreign is better
than a clear view of the clouds.

"Bielsko is
hole!" shouts the punk
with short red hair.
"The rain gets lost.
Its shadow marries sidewalk."

Letter from the Last Place on Earth

Nothing ever happens here
except the weather:
monotonous clouds
with their monotonous
shadows on the fields.
When the rain falls
it leaves us wet
with bewilderment
that it still cares
enough to find us.
Each winter the snow
is late in coming,
apologizes, then quickly
loses us as we drift
in our own footprints
and forget where we are.
North, south, east, west
all become one direction—
final, last, dead end.

And how tired the sun
is when it finally arrives.
Stretching its long arms
over the low hills, the sun
has been known to yawn
at our expense. Delaying
morning for hours until
time becomes as obsolete
as a broken watch and
we feel stranded
on the edge of a dated
map. A map that shows
you can't get here
from there; it's beyond
your reach, your field
of vision. So forget
about visiting and just
write. Don't worry,
your letter will get here
long before the wind does.

Huge Oak Filling the Sky
Mazury, Poland

Here under this umbrella
of green where every speck
of sunlight is overtaken
by leaf and branch and knotted
trunk, the rolling field
of tall grass and wild flower
is humbled into long,
hushed shadows. Here, the land
tries to reach the sky
in the nodding head of branches,
the grasping hand of spring leaves
that beckons heaven
to come down to earth
and be still for one small moment:
share the kinship of seed and root,
the secret of young saplings
and their thin green light.

After the War: Purple Flowers
Spilling from the Windows

In Poland, the land takes over everything,
unrelenting in its mission to regenerate
after the war. Fields overrun sidewalks,
train stations, street corners. Purple
flowers spill from the open windows of houses.
Queen Anne's lace reigns supreme in parking
lots. Even the dead in cemeteries are affected:
no neatly trimmed grass here but waves upon
waves of wild flowers. Blue lupine, saffron,
black-eyed Susan, chicory. The dead love
this wildness growing above their bones.
"*Tak, tak,*" they whisper in the hush of the wind
that scatters the soft gossamer of dandelions
into the waiting air. "Yes, yes, take over this place
that was once lost. Cover it in so much color
even the clouds, who've seen everything,
won't know where death lived for so long."

And who can argue with the dead? Not their
thin ghosts or unborn progeny. Not their
exile who returns after the war, stands
bewildered at their graves, hip-deep
in blue-eyed grass, trying to decipher names
that already belong to the earth.

Songs of Sorrow

On Listening to Gorecki's Third Symphony

I have been searching for you all day,
son/daughter, my sparrow, my lost one.
The wind tells me you're dead and far away,

but I still wander the streets of Zakopane
looking for the Gestapo cell, your last home.
I have been searching for you all day.

You scratched a prayer on the wall, as if to say,
"Mother, mother, do not let me be alone."
The wind tells me you're dead and far away,

but I can't believe it. Not now, not today.
Not even Mary could believe that death of her Son.
I have been searching for you all day,

all night—in the quiet memory of lullaby
that lives in earth, water, moon, sun.
The wind tells me you're dead and far away,

and I am left with nothing but the sound of gray:
deep, convoluted, as it sings to my heart like stone.
I have been searching for you all day;
the wind tells me you're dead and far away.

Chapel with Skulls

Czermna, Poland

Not even the mass graves at Katyń
or the empty crematorium at Auschwitz
can prepare you for this. Gruesome
double helix of skulls and crossbones
rising from the floor, overtaking the wall,
and not stopping until it reaches
the ceiling—overwhelming any angel
or saint that gets in its way.

Truth and justice: that's what the timid
cherub stuck in back with one wing
attempts to convey amidst all this bad news.
But who can blame him for wanting to give up?
In this dark alcove with no windows,
the only light that can find your eye
reflects off the yellowed femur in front of you.
We know this is how we'll all end up:
in the suburbs of America, we don't want to be reminded;
in the heart of Europe, they can't seem to forget.

Moje Rozwiane Włosy

Beyond any control of the East/West border,
Oder/Neisse line, the arbitrary demarcations
of free market and fixed economy, my hair
has become a wild, electric halo that refuses
to be tamed by brush or comb, barrette or clip.
Nimbus of mixed color: deep brown of my mother,
gray of my father, tentative blond of my sister.
All tangled and awry with a history it doesn't
even know. History of peasant women bent
in the fields, of early death in whitewashed huts,
of pogroms, of ghettos, the cut hair of countless
women at Auschwitz—all reduced to the same gray/
blue/black because the gas not only killed but
negated hair pigment. History of Nazi murder
and Stalinist terror, history of the immigrant
and the ones left behind. Snarled, tangled,
caught in the branches of the nearest birch tree.
Dark hair of soft armpit, sturdy leg, hidden
pubis. Hair of the dead cells of history,
flowing like white-water rapids. A river
marking the frontier between two countries—
past and present—that only occasionally shout
a greeting to each other. My hair, my wild hair,
wanting to be a braided rope that connects the two.

Our Last Day in Kraków

Young woman dressed in total black,
only her face and small hands emerge
from this exile of darkness. She is turned
to the wall in the cloister that surrounds
Wawel Castle. Hands outstretched, eyes
closed, her body swaying in prayer.
Is she Moslem, facing Mecca to the east
where the prophet's Kaaba rises like a die
cast from heaven? Is she Jewish, facing Oświęcim
to the west, where Auschwitz and Birkenau
stain the earth: twins of evil catechism,
the serial killer's patron saints?

On the other side of town in the market square,
it's all business—no praying here. Two
live models in the window of a posh boutique:
two trapped beauties imprisoned in blond,
short black leather, thigh-high boots.
Perfectly still for the crowd, for the lone
man who whistles low and wants only
to screw them in front of everybody.

You ask me: what do these women—
the holy and the profane—have in common?
And I reply: the stars and the moon,
the air and the earth, the river and silence,
everything and nothing. How else to explain
the hand of God existing amidst the closing
door of the crematorium, the raw thrust
of the rapist's sole intent? How else
to forgive ourselves for being nothing more,
nothing less than ourselves? Bystanders,
collaborators, hands covered in ash and perfume.

Amber Necklace from Gdańsk

for Lisel Mueller

I don't want the luxury of diamond, luster
of pearl, nor the predictable news of my birth-
stone: emerald, green symbol of love
and success. No sapphires either—no matter
what the ancient Persians said about the blue gem
being responsible for the sky and the ocean.
No jade stone of heaven or picture jasper cave.
I don't want gold or silver, marcasite's northern France.

Give me the prehistoric past that washed ashore
after a storm on the Baltic coast. Fossilized
pine resin that's trapped ancient air. Tears
of the sun that smell like honey, three
strands of the past braided around my neck.
White amber of memory, gold amber of song, dark amber of regret.

IV TO SMILE AT THE CLOSED MOUTH OF LOSS

Colors from the City of White
Photographs from Bielsko-Biała

1

I stand here in a white room
surrounded by photographs of your city.
Small cars crowd the Army Square;
Mickiewicz Street meanders like the poet
and becomes an imposing gray castle. The Pope
freezes his blessing in bronze.
On Listopada Street a thin girl
in blue rushes past, looking
too familiar to be living on the other
side of the world. Where have I
seen her before? Perhaps the fleeting
image trapped in my mirror;
a startled visitor I didn't expect.

2

The woman in purple
fixing her earring.
The woman in red
holding the fresh-cut
gladiolus. Three children
in the country all seated
on the back of the patient
brown horse. Dusk
and the laughing man, empty
fountains framed by an arm,
a solemn woman holding
sliced watermelon. Blond
girl at the beach growing
out of her green
bathing suit. And the white
swans that have followed her
down to the sea.

3

It's not the faces, but the blank
landscape that looks foreign,
exotic. Stretches of damask
plains ending in a blur
of mountains and cloud, they
gossip in a language only
my grandmother could translate.

4

The view from Partyzanci Street
must be a bird's—
or yours, flying away.
Past the silent girl
in the window, her hand
caressing the transparent
curtain. Past the red
streetcar, the uncontrollable
tree that looks like a fern,
the low buildings pretending
to be modern, the hills
dreaming in the background,
wanting to be the sky.

On Winning the Nobel Prize

for Wisława Szymborska

So, where exactly were you when the announcement
was made? When the phone call from Stockholm
jangled the receiver off the hook and placed you
at center of the world—far from the dark velvet
of Kraków where you'd rather be. "Hiking in Zakopane"
was the newspaper's accurate reply—but where?
Certainly not in the village with its cheesy
tourists all carrying authentic walking sticks
and backpacks. Filing past the outdated carnival
on the outskirts, the tiny roads overflowing
with too many cars, too many buses. Even the train
station wouldn't be a good guess, trying to look
invisible next to those too gorgeous mountains.

That's it—the mountains: but which one?
Kasprowy, with its head in the clouds?
Or *Giewont*, where lovers depressed with love
go to fling themselves into the sky? I imagine
you chose neither. I imagine you walked
in the valleys between, making sure to keep
one foot in front of the other until
you reached *Morskie Oko*, eye of the sea,
the largest lake in the Tatras. And at that moment
when the phone rang and your life changed forever,
what you saw was the lake holding the blue
expanse of sky and your thin figure immersed in it.

The Silenced Woman of Kraków

Carved in wooden niches on an elaborate gilded ceiling in the Royal Audience Room of Wawel Castle are thirty life-size heads. Not criminals beheaded for some offense, but medieval celebrities: musicians, artists, poets, philosophers, writers, theologians, and one woman. She is exuberant—as if she's straining to sing—but her mouth is covered with a thick white cloth. Why? Because she was bold enough to come to life for one brief moment and influence the judgment of a king when he wanted to sentence a man to death. She whispered from the ceiling, "Be merciful," and that was enough to change the royal mind (the thief got life, not the executioner's axe) and scare the king half to death. What scared him was not the supernatural occurrence of a talking wooden head, but that he would always be threatened by a second opinion, his noble infallibility questioned, doubted, overturned like a thin piece of paper. So that night, he had her mouth bound shut for good, forever. The one person to clear her throat, speak up, talk back when he least expected it. A woman (for heaven's sake) who probably wouldn't pour her husband a cup of coffee, let alone clean the house. What else to do but put her on the ceiling— freeze her in wood gilded with flecks of gold, azure, burnished orange. Stick her in some castle in Europe, and not just Europe but Eastern Europe (as good as gone and forgotten) like Poland all gray, all sleeping in a cloud, all mist and fog. All silent like hushed women sitting on slow trains that travel from Gdańsk to Zakopane—sea to mountain—and back again.

Twelve Amulets from Medieval Warsaw

We surround ourselves with prayers,
charms, good intentions, constant
bartering to keep the living
alive—the dead, immortal.

Half the hours in a day filled
with the holy legends of twelve apostles:
Peter and his denial
John and his love
Thomas and his doubt
Matthew and his accounts
James and his greatness
the other James and his irrelevance
Bartholomew and his skin
Andrew and his soul
Jude and his hopelessness
Philip and his discretion
Simon and his disguise
Judas and his betrayal.

Half the hours in a day filled
with the universal predictions
of twelve constellations:
Water boy of passion
Fish of reticence
Ram of impulse
Bull of patience
Twins of ambition
Crab of tenderness
Lion of nobility
Virgin of intellect
Scale of sympathy
Scorpion of lust
Archer of imagination
Goat of persistence.

And half a millennium ago, half the hours
in a day filled with the magic
of twelve amulets engraved on a belt

of a Polish knight who refused to die:
against death on a battlefield
against death in a lonely bed
against the evil eye of madness
against the pain of illness
against the loss of memory
against the horror of false wisdom
against the unchaste heart
against the fevered brain
against the closed eye of ignorance
against the open mouth of lies
against all ghosts of the past
against all phantoms of the future.

Twelve legends
twelve predictions
twelve constant petitions
to live forever and ever
módl się za nami
módl się za nami
módl się za nami
pray for us/pray for us/pray for us,
the impatient dead whisper
when we least expect it.

Gospel Eggs

They say the woman from the Ukraine who painted them is crazy. No electricity, no running water. Just her, reading the Bible day in and day out, from Genesis' first crack of light to Revelation's last oblique gleam. And after she reads, she paints. Every day, another egg blown empty with her small breath, another shell painted full of images straight from the mouth of God. He tells her what to paint: flowers, birds, goats, crosses. All surrounded by a concentric chaos. Just like the void before the first day, she says. My friend who is an atheist appreciates her resolve and bought two dozen. He placed them in black egg cartons and enshrined them in his basement among unread books of creative nonfiction and a box filled with every letter he's ever received from anybody. At night, he likes to press the empty eggs to his ear. He never tells me what he hears.

Disposable Icon

My brother-in-law from Ohio
believes it's fate. Fate
that caused the overripe
tomatoes, banana peels, and
coffee grounds in his compost
pile to frame in just-so
photographic irony the discarded
newspaper photo of Terry Anderson.
Gaunt, unshaven, dark-circled—
the ultimate hostage
when hostages were big news
and headline-shattering. Now
the Bosnian Serbs take dozens
of U.N. troops in Bihac
as if they were bargain basement
discount items and hardly
anybody gives a shit.
Which brings us back to irony,
which brings us back to Terry,
and the compost pile
and the perfect picture
my sister's husband snaps
with his Instamatic.
The composition so uncanny
with its squashed reds, bruised
yellows, discarded browns.
Who would believe a famous
face could live here by mere
accident? Staring at the camera
as if everything we do has meaning,
as if nothing we do is important.

Fashion Statement in Front of the
Palace of Culture and Science

If Stalin were still alive, she'd be locked up
with her skintight black leather unitard,
dangling earrings down to there, hair swept
up into an absurdist topknot. She's defiant
as hell and has the tits to prove it:
erect nipples indenting the smooth black.
Not to mention her face, the petulant
scowl for the camera, or that left arm
cocked like a fighter's showing off some
tasty beefcake before the quick jab
lands you on the canvas for the count.
But old Joe's dead and his cold war is over.
Even though that ugly gray monolith
he built after the war as "his eternal
gift" to the people of Warsaw is still
standing: The Palace of Culture
and Science. As if Stalin knew the subtle
nuances of truth and beauty. But she does,
our Polish model slipcased in black,
and she's ready to show it. Steady,
aim, fire. The camera's shot is all
her: who could take their eyes away
from those clenched black leather fists?
Already the building in the background
starts to dismantle itself like someone's fading
memory: facade blurred, main tower gone.
Stalin, dead and impotent, on a bad hair day.

Wedding Gown Bazaar

Warsaw, Poland

Don't look for love
in this wide-angle lens, this
array of beaded lace, crushed chiffon,
neatly trained organza. Unless it's used love,
new for one day then
eventually ordinary like everything else.

An intersection of hanging gowns and dreaming women:
no men in sight. That's what you
discern behind the camera with its

round, open eye, its sense of free
overwhelming light. Who can
blame us for wanting to try it? This
experiment in forever, this too loud
rhapsody of vows, this open-air market dedicated
to finding the right size. Just the right fit.

The Visitors from Warsaw

for Francine Paolini

Sounds like the plot of a Polanski movie—
a story told by an Italian singer from Capri
about a group of Polish Amway distributors.
Don't laugh: Polish Amway distributors visiting America.

A story told by an Italian singer from Capri,
she was entertaining this business group from Warsaw.
Don't laugh: Polish Amway distributors visiting America.
They were in this glitzy ballroom of a swank hotel.

She was entertaining this business group from Warsaw,
when a storm caused all the lights to go out.
They were in this glitzy ballroom of a swank hotel
when the mic went dead. Her amplified voice gone.

When a storm caused all the lights to go out,
no one from Warsaw panicked, they lit candles.
When the mic went dead, her amplified voice gone,
they started to sing in the soft dark with full voices.

No one from Warsaw panicked, they lit candles
and sang about the Vistula *syrena,* Tatra *śnieg,* Jesus in Bethlehem.
They started to sing in the soft dark with full voices
and serenaded the Italian from Capri.

And sang about the Vistula *syrena,* Tatra *śnieg,* Jesus in Bethlehem,
the beautiful girls in Kraków, their dead mothers in Gdańsk,
and serenaded the Italian from Capri
with love songs and polkas and heavy-beat *oberki,*

the beautiful girls in Kraków, their dead mothers in Gdańsk,
and they didn't stop—even when the lights came back on—
with love songs and polkas and heavy-beat *oberki.*
These visitors from Warsaw who sell American soap.

And they didn't stop—even when the lights came back on
and the Italian singer finally found her voice—
these visitors from Warsaw who sell American soap
but couldn't stop singing about the country they left.

Even when the Italian singer finally found her voice
and the mic drowned out the mermaid, the snow, and Jesus,
they couldn't stop singing about the country they left.
Sounds like the plot of a Polanski movie.

Dancing with My Sister

for Deborah

We're not talking those crazy Polish weddings
in Cleveland, where we both learned how to dance,
clutching each other's sweaty hands, galloping
to the Beer Barrel Polka, and trying not to bump
into Uncle Johnnie and his whirling Chicago Hop.

This is now, tonight, in a smoky bar in Detroit
where two women dancing together can scandalize
any pimp within range. Where the hotshot
bartender can mix anything and has the wide eyes
to prove it: bloody mary, wallbanger, a zombie
with a spike of lime that will raise the dead.

Above the crowded dance floor, in the maze
of catwalks, the geek of a lighting man
(who reminds us of every boy in high school
who fast-danced with his hands behind his back)
shines the spotlight right on us. And we glow.

Girl, do we glow. Not for the memory of those
distant high school boys whose faces we can't
remember. Not for the fluid desire ebbing
around us on the floor and beyond where silent
men sit in the dark. We glow for the raw truth
of Aretha's voice spelling out RESPECT;
for the way our hair curls down past our shoulders;
for our legs that can outdance any young thing;
for the miracle that we survived our childhoods—
mother's obsessive cleaning, father's factory shifts,
the Erwin Street mob of pre-juvenile delinquents.
We glow because we came from the same burnt-out dream
of second-generation immigrants and learned to smile
at the closed mouth of loss and dance, dance, dance.